T0130506

Alive and Running

*From fat to fit in 16 diet-free weeks thru the
safe enjoyment of running*

George C. Erkmann

 www.trafford.com

North America & international
toll-free: 1 888 232 4444 (USA & Canada)
fax: 812 355 4082

Dedicated to my wife,

Maureen Ann Erkmann

...Whose love, patience and understanding
have added more years to my life, and
more life to my years.

"A jogger jogs for his health. A runner will run if it kills him"

Dr. Gabe Mirkin

"You haven't failed until you've stopped trying"

Eleanore Roosevelt

Contents

Why Run?

"I have a weight problem ".
*"**You** have a weight problem ? ".*
*"Yes. I have to eat 4000 calories a day or I'll lose
   weight"*

Why *do* I run? I have more reasons now than when I first started. I wanted health and longevity. Today I run because it raises the quality of my life.

By quality of life I mean that:
* I eat what I want without gaining weight.
* I sleep like a log.
* I have plenty of energy for work and for play
* I hardly ever get sick.
* My blood pressure has stayed at 110/70,
* I don't need prescription, or over the counter drugs.

I can work, play touch-tackle, iceskate, backpack, canoe and dance for hours without requiring a day of recuperation or a follow up visit to a doctor. I outlast my children and grandchildren in any of these activities and, in return, earn their respect and admiration.

Three months after I started my exercise program I noticed a marked increase in my endurance, and some unexpected bonuses. I lost most of my "Type A" personality characteristics. Waiting at a red light, a line at the bank or post office, was no longer a source of annoyance. My friends noticed and wondered at my calmer demeanor.

The bottom line was that I just felt good; because -
*"**It's not days of your life, but the life in your days that counts**."*

1

In The Beginning ...

I grew up in Queens, a borough of New York City, when Queens had many ball fields, empty lots, and streets void of traffic. We played stick-ball, baseball, touch football, and other physically active games. Exercise was integral to all of my activities.

In my teens, I carried golf bags, delivered groceries, and on weekends, I drove a milk truck and distributed 1100 quarts of milk in less than four hours. These jobs kept me in great physical condition and, although I had a healthy appetite, I had very little body fat.

After college I got an office job. For exercise I walked to the coffee and doughnut table, and the company cafeteria.

I retained my (now) unhealthy appetite, and my excess calories went to body fat. In two years I gained 20 pounds. I began to resemble a doughnut, round and soft in the middle. No surprise; after all, we are what we eat! I ignored my de-conditioned state until two men in my office died of cardiac arrest. One was 45 and the other 51. Both men were overweight. That was my wake-up call.

I tried dieting, and lost weight, but as soon as the diet ended the lost pounds reappeared almost instantly. At the time I didn't know that diet without exercise never works. I didn't know that a diet slows the metabolic rate, the rate at which a body burns calories. It's the body's instinctive protection against starvation. When you resume your normal diet your slow metabolism tells the body to put back those lost pounds. Repeated cycles of this behavior is known as popularly known as "yo-yo dieting."

When I was a kid, I stayed thin, while I ate everything in sight. It was then I realized that the only difference between "me-the-kid" and "me-the-adult" was that the adult "me" wasn't moving. "Aha!" I said, "I need exercise." But which exercise, and how much?

Seek and Ye Shall Find

While I was looking for answers, so was Dr. Kenneth Cooper, an Air Force Physiologist. His job was to keep Air Force personnel in top physical condition. He needed answers to the questions "How much should a person exercise?" and "Which exercise provides the most benefit for the least amount of time?" He conducted a study and published his results in a book entitled "Aerobics".

Cooper tested hundreds of Air Force volunteers on treadmills. He also tested civilians and world class athletes. His test data showed that endurance and cardiac fitness was a function of the amount of oxygen consumed per second, per pound of body weight. In other words, the best conditioned athletes could consume oxygen at a very high rate.

Dr. Cooper might have completed his study with a report submitted to JAMA, full of medical jargon and understood only by doctors and, perhaps he did. But his book, "Aerobics" is a service to mankind, and if I was on the Nobel Prize committee, Dr. Cooper would be my nominee. His book presents many practical plans for attaining excellent physical conditioning.

Dr. Cooper's book describes ...
   ...how to evaluate your present physical condition and
      how to **gradually** improve your physical condition by...
            ...walking
            ...running
            ...biking
            ...swimming
            ...tennis and many other physical activities

The activity I chose was running.

...

My initial efforts combined walking interspersed with short bursts of very slow running, four times a week. After twelve weeks, I could run two miles, very slowly, without stopping to walk. As I gradually increased my mileage, my weight dropped, my cholesterol count went down, along with my rest pulse rate, and blood pressure. My endurance for work and play increased substantially.

Meanwhile, my nine year old daughter, Jeanne, was running races with her school team. Jeanne's coach was a retired U.S. Army Captain and he conned the parents into running in an age group race. He called us his "Over the Hill Team". There were two age groups: 16 to 39 and 40 and over. I was two weeks short of my 40th birthday, so I had to compete with the younger group, but I finished in the middle of the pack and got hooked on competitive racing.

I increased my weekly mileage, quickened my pace, and entered race after race. In small fields I'd place an occasional second or third and, once in a while, a I'd win. I joined my company's athletic club so that I could run at lunchtime. I was now a member of the running community.

Then a co-worker, only ten years my senior, died of a heart attack during a lunch-time run. Another was hit by a car and his right leg smashed from ankle to hip. Two biking friends were run over and one died. I had better luck; now and then a muscle tear, a pulled tendon, who could complain about that?

After my co-worker died, my company threatened to shut us down. I realized that our injuries were a result of our own carelessness, and in an effort to prevent a shutdown of our company gym, I wrote and distributed a set of safety rules. That was the beginning of this book. The first edition was published in 1980. I've learned much since then, and I hope to pass on what I've learned to you.

**Stepping Out on Deadly Streets: Pedestrian fatalities
rose 24% last year**   The New York Daily News
By Dave Saltonstall Feb 8, 1998

In the never ending stand-off between New York City
motorists and the pedestrians who dodge them, one number overshadows all else: Every 37 minutes, another
pedestrian gets hit by a driver somewhere in the five
 boroughs.

Thirty-nine times a day, with terrifying regularity, police
rush to the scene of yet another crash between man and
motorist, New York State Department of Motor Vehicles
records show.

"The chances of being killed by someone in a car in this
city are now far greater than getting killed by a stranger
with a weapon," said John Kaehny, executive director of
Transportation Alternatives, a pedestrian and bicyclist
rights group. "That's the grim reality."

Source: New York City Police Department

**The above is an excerpt from the New York Daily News
Published on February 8. 1998**

Note that "pedestrians" includes runners *and* walkers and that
New York City includes the boroughs of Queens and Staten
Island, which are less densely populated than Manhattan.
the Bronx and Brooklyn

Is'nt Running Dangerous?

Headline: _"Jogger Dies on Track"_
William Thomas, a freshman at Central High School, collapsed and died while jogging on the track. Harold Thomas, William's father, said " My son was in perfect health..."

This story appeared in our local newspaper. I've changed the names of the people and the school, but the story is true. Had I known only what I read, I would have wondered how a healthy boy could die so tragically, and concluded that running was a dangerous activity.

But I knew more than the newspaper reported, because I was an active parent at William's school . He wanted to lose weight to be under the limit for the wrestling team. He fasted for three days, and abstained from drinking water. On the third day, which was very hot and humid, William donned a sweat suit, a rubber suit over the sweat suit, and proceeded to run around the track. The actual cause of death was cardiac arrest brought on by his heart's desperate attempt to cool his body under conditions of extreme heat.

Headline: _"Jogger Struck by Car; Condition Critical"_
Albert Smith, 35, a resident of Centerville, was struck by a car driven by Lawrence Chambers while running on route 141. "I came over the top of the hill", said Chambers, " and there he was, running in the right lane. I jammed on my brakes but there was no way I could stop in time. He probably didn't hear my horn because he was wearing a headset."

Another true story. Why did this happen? Smith was running with his back to traffic, in the right lane, on the other side of a hill,out of sight of the driver, and the only sense that might have warned him, his hearing, was otherwise occupied.

When a runner gets hurt, usually the fault of the runner.

To quote the comic strip character Pogo:
"We have met the enemy, and he is us".

Can Anybody Run?

E veryone should have a yearly physical. Without a physical there is no chance of early detection, and the first symptom of cancer or heart disease may be pain or sudden death.

If you do not have yearly physicals there may be some condition of which you're unaware, that would make it inadvisable to run. Even if you believe your health is good, you should have a complete physical, including a stress test. Find a doctor who is in good physical condition and ask him what he does for exercise. If he's overweight and tells you that running is dangerous, find another doctor. (My internist runs regularly and has a "NY Marathon Finisher" certificate framed on the wall in his office.)

The aforementioned advice is given not because I'm smarter than you, its because like most people, I learn "the hard way". I decided to take a stress test after a bad experience at the finish of a two mile race. I was winning with only 20 yards to go, when a competitor started to pass me. A voice within me said *"no way".* I picked up the pace, and won by a couple of feet. I immediately felt faint and stupid at the same time. This was my first and unplanned stress test but wondered what would have happened had I failed it.

An optional stress test can be expensive, but if you complain about "symptoms" your medical plan will probably cover the cost,

Assuming that you're physically qualified to run it's time to consider your running equipment

Running shoes

R unning shoes are different from tennis, basketball, handball, and boat sneakers. It's tempting to go out on your first run wearing your old basketball sneakers. This is a mistake, because if you start running in the wrong shoes, the chances are good that you'll get hurt and conclude that running is not for you. There are some who can run 20 miles in army boots with no ill effects, but they are rare individuals.

Most of us have structural imperfections that will bring on aches and pains when we start to pile on the miles. Good running shoes, properly fitted, will provide adequate protection against injury and in some cases, compensation for conditions such as flat feet which cause the ankles to turn inward (pronate.)

You should buy your running shoes from a local store where the people who own the business are runners. The Super Runner stores in Manhattan and Long Island are owned by Gary Murcke, the winner of the 1977 New York City Marathon. His employees are runners, and can recommend the best shoe for the individual. Most of the major cities in the US have stores like Gary's. Don't buy running shoes from a big department store where dress shoes and athletic shoes are all grouped together in one section of the store. The chances are good the sales people won't be runners.

There are two categories of running shoes; training shoes and racing flats. Racing flats are meant for short races, are very light and don't provide enough support or cushioning for longer distances. The majority of runners use training shoes for everyday running and racing. Runner's World Magazine used to rate shoes for quality but they lost advertising revenue from the manufacturers who didn't come out on top in their ratings. Now every Fall, they list shoes by price and suitability for a variety of runners and running styles (pronators, supinators, heavy runners, light runners etc.)

8

It's all about you

R unning shoes are so comfortable that almost anything you try on will feel good. Be patient and don't plunk down your money on the first pair you try. In some stores they'll let you go out for a test run. I've done this many times, but once I was chased by the owner and his assistant. They didn't catch me, and when I returned to the store I pointed out that I had left my wallet on the counter. They were unhappy; probably because they couldn't catch me

You may find a shoe that hasn't been rated. If it feels good on your feet and the price is right, try rating it for yourself.
Look at the drawing below.

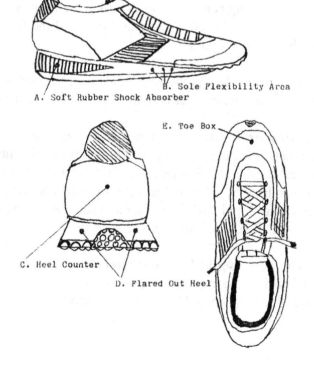

A. Soft Rubber Shock Absorber
B. Sole Flexibility Area
C. Heel Counter
D. Flared Out Heel
E. Toe Box

Running shoe Technology

Heel Cushion   Look at the area under the heel. There should be a wedge of soft rubber (A) between the sole and the upper part of the shoe. This material must be soft and spongy to effectively absorb shock. It should yield fairly easily if you stick your thumb in it. The elevation of this wedge near the rear of the shoe protects the Achilles tendon from overstretching. (Racing flats do not have this wedge and a half-mile race experience with racing flats rewarded me with two weeks of Achilles Tendonitis.)

Sole Flexibility   Grasp the heel of the shoe firmly in one hand, then with the other hand try to bend the shoe in half by pulling the toe up and back towards the heel (B.) This should be easy but can be difficult with a poor quality shoe. With insufficient sole flexibility you may develop pain on the ball of your foot. If your current pair of running shoes fails this test, you can increase sole flexibility by slicing across the soles with a razor or by drilling a number of holes in the sole area near the ball of the foot. (Don't do this while wearing your shoes.)

Heel Stability Ankles can be easily turned if the heel of the shoe is unstable. There are two characteristics of a stable heel:

1. **A firm heel counter**, which is the upper rear part of the shoe that holds the heel in place (C.) If the heel counter is soft and mushy, the foot can slide laterally off the sole of the shoe resulting in a twisted ankle. Grasp the heel counter between your thumb and forefinger and squeeze. There should be a high degree of stiffness and support.

2. **The heel should flare out laterally** from under the shoe (D.) This is the complete opposite of the most unstable heel in existence, the spike heel found on women's dress shoes.

The Toe Box should be rounded and roomy. Some of the highest rated running shoes are defective in this area by providing a narrow toe box. A common running injury Is "black toe", a condition in which toenails blacken and fall off. This is caused by the pinching of the toenails between the inside of the toe box and the top of the foot.

When your foot strikes the ground, your shoe momentarily stops moving, but your foot continues to move forward, inside the shoe, until the front of the toe hits the front of the toe box. The skin on top of the foot behind the toenail continues to move. The toenail is pinched for an instant between the front of the toe box and the skin behind the toe nail. The pinching results in bleeding under the toe nail, i.e. "black toe."

You can avoid "black toe" by lacing your shoes so that the first two eyelets at the bottom of each shoe are unused. When the lace is pulled tight, the toe box will be roomier with no loss of support.

The sole of the shoe is designed to for a variety of surfaces; concrete, macadam and dirt. It provides shock absorption in addition to that already built into the shoe. Running in worn soles will hurt you.

Given a length of twenty inches from sole to knee, and a heel width of three inches, a quarter inch displacement on the outside of the heel could cause a 3-1/3 inch horizontal displacement on the knee. (If you did well in Geometry, you can verify this.) The ankle is flexible and compensates for some of this displacement, but the stress is there just the same. Running with worn heels can injure your knees and lower legs.

My Shoes are wearing out ...

It seems like you just bought these shoes and they're already showing signs of wear. . Do you have to buy a new pair?

Early shoe wear occurs on the outside corner of the heel. You can patch this area with rubber cement or Shoe Patch. These products have the consistency of peanut butter and dry to a hard rubber-like compound after a few hours. It takes ten minutes to do a light re-building which will last for 50 miles. A piece of tape will keep the soft patch material from overflowing the edges of the heel. Removing the tape after the patch material dries is optional..

You should have a second pair of shoes for use while your patch-work is drying. Alternating days between two pairs of shoes allows the soles time to decompress from your previous run.

Your shoes will last longer if you wash them. Salt from sweat weakens rubber and corrodes stitching. A strong laundry detergent , a stiff brush and a bucket of warm water will get rid of the heavy dirt. Then, when your wife isn't looking, put them in the washing machine and hang them up to dry. They'll look and feel like new.

The thin removable insoles that come with the shoes provide no shock absorption. I remove the insoles from my new shoes and insert shock absorbing insoles which reduce the effects of repeated impact and provide better foot support. You can buy these insoles from running shoe stores or from roadrunnersports.com. The insoles will extend the life of your shoes until the tops get soft; then it's time to buy new shoes..

Don't discard your old shoes. They'll be good enough to wear around the house, in your yard, or when shopping, and charities will accept your old shoes for the homeless or other needy groups, but please wash them before you donate them.

The Emergency Kit– Part I

An Identification Tag is an essential part of your running gear. If you're found unconscious and alone, the attending EMS person needs to know who to contact, your blood type, rest pulse, and any allergic reactions you may have.

The rest pulse is included because highly conditioned athletes have very low rest pulse rates. Winning marathon runners, and champion tennis players, have rest pulse rates in the low 30's . A low pulse rate in a sedentary person is a symptom of shock, a dangerous condition requiring immediate treatment.

When training for a marathon, my rest pulse has been as low as 39.   I know of two cases where doctors wanted to treat an injured runner for shock. Both runners were conscious and tried to tell the doctor that their pulse rate was normally low but they weren't believed. An ID bracelet that reads *"Runner; Normal rest pulse in the low 40's"* is more credible than the mumbling of an injured and semi-conscious person.

People with special medical problems, wear "Medic Alert" bracelets in case of an emergency. Medic Alert was founded by Dr. Marion Collins after his daughter almost died from a reaction to an antitoxin sensitivity test.

A Medic Alert bracelet is engraved with the world recognized Medic Alert Symbol, a critical message and a collect phone number which can be called, 24 hours a day, for access to more detailed patient data. There's a one time registration fee for the bracelet and a small annual contribution. I've worn my bracelet 24/7 for years.

It reads: *"Runner; Normal Pulse in the low forties;*
Blood type A pos. "
plus my ID, and Medic Alert's phone number.

The Emergency Kit—Part 2

It was a beautiful Summer evening. I'd finished a salad, two helpings of lasagna and a glass of wine. My daughter Jeanne arrived home. She hadn't eaten dinner.

"Hey Dad, let's go for a run."
"I can't run now; I just finished dinner."
"You promised!"

I would never run after eating a heavy meal, and the last and only promise I ever made, and kept, was to love, honor and obey. Well...love and honor. Two out of three isn't bad.

"If I run now I'll leave my dinner on the road."
"Come on, we'll run slow."

After slogging a mile, my side-stitch and indigestion began to abate.

"Hey Jeanne, there's a picnic at Hempstead Harbor Park and it's only eight miles from here. We can grab a ride home."
"Ok dad"

After two miles, Jeanne turned to me and said,
"I don't feel so good. I'm going home"
"Hey, you dragged me out here and now you're quitting?"
"I don't want to go to the park, I'm going home."

We parted. I like to finish what I start. Well … not everything, but I've never quit a run.

Seven miles later, I arrived at the park. The sun had set and the only light was from the glowing coals of barbeque pits. I was sweat soaked, thirsty and an evening feast for hordes of mosquitoes.
I had to find my friends. I didn't want to run home in the dark.

I approached some silhouettes huddled around a fire and called...

"Walter.. Bob"
"No Walter or Bob here."

Read the last three sentences ten times.
"They must have left early. What now?"

I spotted a public phone booth (I didn't have a cell phone) and re-trieved a quarter from my head band . I wear a headband when I run. The headband is a hollow tube. If you cut a small slit on the in-side layer you can insert a sandwich bag containing coins and bills. I always stuff my headband with money in case I have to call for help..

I needed help.
"Hello, Maureen?"
"Where are you?"

"I'm at Hempstead Harbor Park. Walter and Bob have left and I was wondering if you'd come and pick me up."
"Pause"

"We'll stop for ice cream."
"I'll be there in twenty minutes."

It could have been worse. There was an ultra-marathoner who went for a run on a beautiful Summer night and when he called his wife in the morning, he was 125 miles from home. She drove to meet him. I'll bet it cost him more than ice cream.

Starting ...

Periodically review your goals. Initially they may be health oriented, but you'll also find that regular, vigorous exercise, well planned and executed, will vastly improve the quality of your life.

Exercise should be part of your lifestyle; missed if skipped. It should be enjoyable, and never endanger your health or safety.

The chart that follows is an excerpt from Dr. Cooper's book. It's a starting program for a healthy person between 30 and 39 years of age. The program for persons 50 to 59 is almost identical except that it starts with a one mile instead of two, and the times are slower.

After completing week twelve, you will be earning over 60 points per week, a high level of aerobic fitness. You can maintain this level, or if you want more, you can continue increasing your distance and decreasing your pace.

Running/Jogging Exercise Program
(30-39 Years of Age)

Week	Activity	Distance (miles)	Time Goal (minutes)	Freq./Wk	Points/wk
1	walk	2.0	34:00	3	12.2
2	walk	2.5	42:00	3	16.3
3	walk	3.0	50:00	3	20.4
4	walk/jog	2.0	25:00	4	26.4
5	walk/jog	2.0	24:00	4	28.0
6	jog	2.0	22:00	4	31.6
7	jog	2.5	20:00	4	36.0
8	jog	2.5	26:00	4	43.7
9	jog	2.5	25:00	4	46.0
10	jog	3.0	31:00	4	53.7
11	jog	3.0	29:00	4	57.6
12	jog	3.0	27:00	4	61.3

... and Maintaining

R un at least three times, preferably four to six times per week. Allow a day of rest to rebuild sore muscles and to replenish muscle glycogen. Running seven days a week can quickly become drudgery, make you mentally and physically stale, and lead to injury and illness.

For three runs a week, spread out your run days (e.g., Wednesday, Friday and Sunday.) For six runs per week, three days on, one day off, and three days on. It's not good to cram all your exercise into a weekend. Dr. Simon Rabkin of the University of Manitoba found that 75% of fatal heart attacks that occur on the job, occur on Monday and of those that occur at home, 47% occur on Monday. Monday's events are a delayed reaction to what you did on Saturday and Sunday.

If you haven't run for two weeks or more, don't resume at the level you were at when you stopped. Resume at a slower pace and lower mileage. You can de-condition quickly. Like all physical systems, the body reacts badly to sudden change.

Some day, you may be tempted to run a marathon . Finishing a 26.2 mile race will enhance your self image and impress friends and family. A friend will convince you that it's "no big deal"; he's going to do it, and "...we'll train together."

Friends have talked me into running marathons and then have quit during training, leaving me committed to finishing something I didn't intend to start. I've run thirty-eight marathons with and without friends. Avoid the temptation until you have a year or two under your belt, and are able to complete 12 weeks of training from a base of 40 miles a week.

Your Daily Run

B efore you run, take ten minutes to stretch your leg muscles. Stretching loosens tight muscles and helps prevent injury. Most of the runners I know don't take the time to stretch, but it's a small investment of time and worth the effort. The times that I got injured were usually those times when I neglected to stretch before my run.

Why should you stretch? When you are sitting still or lying in bed, your muscle fibers contract (shorten). If you're over 40, and you've been sitting for a long lunch or meeting, your legs may feel stiff when you leave your seat. If you start from rest, and immediately break into a sprint, you risk a muscle or tendon pull.

Stretching should be done *very slowly.* Stretches that incorporate bouncing or fast action are known as ballistic stretches and can do more harm than good. The idea is to *warm up* the muscles before use. Move in slow motion, followed by very slow stretches.

Some runners, especially when racing, go from a standstill to a fast running pace and feel terrible during the early part of their run. Working muscles demand 4 to 5 times the oxygen they need at rest, but sudden increased demands on the heart and circulatory system results in a lag between supply and demand for the entire race.

But, you say, *"If I don't start fast, I won't run my best time".* That's true. So before you start, do a slow run as a warm up so that your body won't go into shock when the gun goes off. A fast start will use a disproportionate amount of glycogen (muscle fuel) and if the race is long, your fuel will be expended before you finish. When you run out of muscle fuel, you stiffen up and slow down, an occurrence that runners call **"Hitting the wall"** and bikers call **"Bonking."** (See the chart on the next page)

There will be variations in the way you feel from day to day. You should expect this. We all have physical and emotional highs and lows which affect all phases of life including the way we run. There were days when I didn't want to run, so I'd take off my watch and run at slower than normal pace. On these days I felt better at the end of the run than I did at the beginning. Before you run any races, take a stress test to insure your coronary arteries are clear.

After you run, warm down gradually. Jog slowly, then walk and continue walking for a few minutes. Sudden changes are a shock to the human body. A transition from a fast run to sitting or lying down, can result in dizziness or fainting. (If you ride horses, the stable will require you to walk the horse after you dismount.) After running your leg muscles will be tight. After you warm down, stretch to prevent soreness.

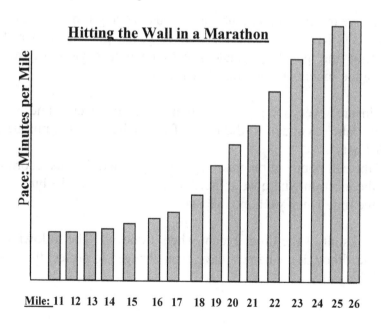

Hitting the Wall in a Marathon

Pace: Minutes per Mile

Mile: 11 12 13 14 15 16 17 18 19 20 21 22 23 24 25 26

Are You OK? ...Are You OK?

I've run marathons in Boston, Jersey Shore, Long Island, New York and Washington DC. I believe the New York City Marathon is the best organized of the aforementioned. Typically, 60 thousand runners start, 95 percent finish and, on the next day, everyone who crossed the finish line in under seven hours, can see their finish time listed accurately in the New York Times. This is made possible by. thousands of volunteers who score the race, dispense water, direct traffic, and provide medical assistance.

Imagine that you're one of the 3000 medical volunteers on Marathon Day . You've donated a day of your life to help runners, most of whom finish fatigued, sweaty, dehydrated, and barely able to walk. You want to be useful. The true story that follows is an example of the attention and care provided runners by the NYC Marathon .

Every year our running club rents a bus to bring runners to and from the NYC Marathon. There are three goals: get the runners to the starting line, get the spectators to Manhattan to view the race, and bring the runners home after they finish

To insure everyone gets a ride home, we give each runner a water-proof label to attach to the back of his or her running number. The label lists...
....the cell phone numbers of the bus driver and the bus coordinator.
....the location where we'll meet before we return to the bus.
...the time when we hope to leave for home.

It works all of the time, except when it doesn't. The following story is true although the names have been changed to protect the innocent and the guilty.

"Everyone is here except Patrick"
"He was ahead of me ...he should have finished by now"
"I saw him being carried into the medical tent"

I tried to get to the medical tent but the security guard would not let me into the finish area. He relented when I told him about Patrick. I found Patrick lying on a cot, an IV in each arm and an oxygen mask covering his nose and mouth. He was conscious, so I asked him...

"Pat! What happened? What's wrong?"
"Nothing"
"What do you mean- "nothing"?
"Everyone kept asking me if I was OK? I kept saying "yes"; I was getting tired of saying "yes", so I told them I felt a little pressure in my chest at mile 22. They threw me on a stretcher and carried me in here."

"How do you feel now?"
"I feel great; I finished the race feeling good"

I asked the nurse to release Patrick so we could take him home. She answered "No, he's going to the hospital"

Then she asked me "Are you OK?" I said, "I need a psychiatrist" "We have one; she said, "come with me." She grabbed my arm but I broke free and ran .

We found Patrick in one of the three local hospitals.
One of us claimed to be his uncle and he was released .
A few days later Patrick got a hospital bill for $880.

You Are What You Eat

Y ou've heard that the average American's diet is heavily loaded with fat and sugar and is greatly in need of reform. Yet an "Ideal" Diet would not work for everyone. A sedentary person needs very little carbohydrate intake, and a very active person needs a lot.

People don't change their eating habits unless they have a great incentive to do so. If your lifestyle has progressed from sedentary to active, you will change your diet or your performance will suffer. Mike, who was 100 pounds overweight, lost those extra pounds by dieting strictly on protein and by walking, and later, running. After he started running, Mike felt sluggish and unenergetic. He was burning more calories, but he was still on a high protein diet. His energy increased when he started to phase carbohydrates (runner's fuel) into his diet.

Here's a list of "do's and don'ts" summarized from a study of diets for active people. These are general rules that work for most runners but, as always there are exceptions.

- Run on an empty stomach and empty colon. A cup of caffeinated coffee will help to empty the colon within an hour of ingestion.

- Protein and fat are hard to digest. Meat will remain in the stomach for as long as 10 hours. Carbohydrates are digested quickly.

- Avoid eating for at least four hours before you run. The fuel you'll need for running is already in your system. New intake will only keep the digestive system busy diverting blood from the muscle system to the stomach.

- Avoid high fat intake. Fat remains in the bloodstream 12 to 14 hours after ingestion. It coats the oxygen-carrying red corpuscles causing them to clump together and impedes their passage through the capillaries. That will slow you down!

.

Oxygen transfer can be reduced by as much as 30 percent. A breakfast of bacon and eggs (75% fat) is one of the worst pre-exercise meals you can eat.

- Sugar, honey and other simple carbohydrates should be treated with caution. It's all in the timing. If you ingest sugar hours before your run, your blood sugar will quickly rise and the body will react by pouring insulin into the blood stream to process what appears to be an abnormally high rate of sugar intake. An overshoot of insulin will occur, thereby processing all the sugar just ingested plus whatever was already in your bloodstream. The result is a lower-than-normal blood sugar, a weak washed-out feeling and a hunger for more sugar; initiating a yo-yo cycle.

- Sugar ingested during a run can be beneficial because insulin action is suppressed during exercise. Again caution is the watchword. If the weather is hot, you'll ingest more fluids and sugar causes fluid retention in the stomach and slows the passage of water to your sweat glands. Large intakes of sweet fluid during hot weather may result in stomach cramps.

- A vegetarian can only fulfill nutritional needs if meals are carefully planned. You can get protein from a vegetarian diet but only if four of the eight essential amino acids are ingested within 30 minutes of each other. Populations where meat is scarce have learned to combine whole grain cereals with milk, rice with beans or sesame seeds. and thereby get the essential amino acids. Without red meat it's difficult to get enough vitamin B12 and populations low in B12 are often susceptible to anemia. Anyone considering vegetarianism, should read a few books on the subject before changing a diet.

"Never again"… "Never again"
Post race comments from an anonymous marathon runner.

Getting an Edge

It was a bad day to run a marathon. The day was hot and humid and everyone's predicted finish time was off by at least a half hour; mine by forty minutes.

On the bus ride home, I was sitting between two runners, my head swiveling back and forth, as if I was watching a tennis match, as they took turns saying "Never again",…"Never again". Two weeks later the three of us were training for another marathon. The mind represses the memory of pain, and our bad day, and the resolve to "give it up forever", was quickly forgotten.

No one I know feels comfortable after finishing a marathon and much of the discomfort is due to the loss of muscle fuel (glycogen), without which, a runner's legs get stiff and almost immobile. A trained runner normally stores enough glycogen for 18 miles after which the symptom known as "Hitting-the-Wall" takes place. A runner can "hit the wall" before 18 miles if he starts too fast or if he hasn't trained properly.

One way to delay, or even avoid, hitting the wall is to overload your muscles with glycogen using a technique known as "Carbohydrate Loading" (or Carbo Loading) This is done during the week before the marathon through diet and running.

Carbo Loading sounds like a normal runner's diet but there's a significant difference. You don't want to *load*, you want to *overload.* Eight days before the race, you start depleting your muscles of glycogen. For the first two or three days you avoid carbs, eating mostly protein. You continue to run as part of the depletion phase. You switch to carbs when you feel depleted (you'll know!). The body senses glycogen deficiency, and compensates by *overloading* depleted leg muscles with glycogen. The diet on the opposite page worked for me. Will it work for you? There's only one way to find out.

Carbohydrate Loading Diet

	Days 7	6	5	Before 4	Marathon 3	2	1	Race Day
	High Protein & Low Carbohydrate			**Low Protein & High Carbohydrate**				
	Glycogen Depletion Phase*			Glycogen Overload Phase				
Breakfast	bacon, ham, Eggs, milk, cheese (no buns, bread, toast, cereal sugar, honey, or Jam) _WATER_ _no bread_			dry cereal, french toast, buns, muffins bananas	oatmeal, bagels, honey raisins, dates, (no meat or cheese) Juice or water	pancakes, doughnuts jam prunes	Big Carbo Breakfast (avoid fats)	Very Light Carbo Breakfast (1 banana or 1 pancake)
Lunch	eggs, cheese, chicken, ham, roast beef, salami avocado cantaloupe watermelon grapefruit _WATER_ _no bread_			yogurt pasta peanut butter bananas pineapple	eggplant herc bread figs, dates oranges Juice or water	pizza rolls persimmons fruit juice	Moderate Lunch (avoid fats)	You're running - Gatorade and water, if it's hot, avoid sugar*
Dinner	steak, tuna, pork, chicken, all beef hot dogs, sausage _no bread_ asparagus cabbage cucumbers lettuce mushrooms sauerkraut squash tomatoes _WATER_ _no bread_ cheesecake			water, pasta lasagna lima beans kidney beans cake,cookies,pie,dates,figs doughnuts	beer, wine, fruit juice pizza noodles corn peas	fruit juice rice potatoes yams	Light Dinner (avoid fats)	Post Race Lots of fluids High Carbo Dinner

* sugar keeps water in the stomach

It Only Hurts When I ...

"You're 43 years old; you shouldn't be running " The doctor's comment surprised me. I had an answer for him, but I didn't think he'd understand. He was easily 30 pounds over-weight and his office reeked of cigarette smoke. I spotted an ash tray on his desk and realized I'd visited the wrong doctor.

I had pulled my right Achilles Tendon racing in a pair of light weight, low-heeled shoes and assumed that an orthopedic special-ist would best know how to heal me. I paid his fee, and left his office with a prescription for an anti-inflammatory drug.

In my local library, I found a book entitled **"Athletic Training and Conditioning" by 0. Dayton.** I expected to find information on training. Instead, the book was full of illustrations of tapings, bandages and splints.

Mr. Dayton was a member of the Coaching Staff of the Yale University Football Team and part of his job was to keep his healthy but sometimes injured players in good repair. His book showed me how to tape my foot to limit the range of motion of my Achilles Tendon. I could run wearing the tape, but was limited to flat terrain In two weeks, I was healed. I never filled the prescription nor did I ever revisit that doctor.

You may wake up in the morning, climb out of bed, and find out that something hurts You're injured but you don't remember getting hurt.. It may be something very subtle, having developed over a period of days, or it might be obvious (e.g. a change of shoes) Usually it will be something you did two days ago. Did you increase the length of your average run? Did you spend your Saturday climbing up and down a ladder? I've kept a Runner's Log which included other physical activities. It's been very useful in helping me understand what I shouldn't do if I want to stay healthy, e.g., climbing ladders.

Most patients in a doctor's waiting room are sedentary. and the doctor seldom sees an injured but physically active adult. The injured runner can usually get better advice from Podiatrists, Physical Therapists, or fellow runners than he can from his general practitioner, that is, unless his doctor, like mine, is a runner..

The longer you delay treatment, the longer it will take to heal. Before you get to the doctor's office, you can start your own treatment by icing and elevating the injured area to reduce swelling.

The proper treatment of an injury includes some form of physical therapy which includes gently exercising the injured member. The exercise serves a dual purpose of preventing atrophy, from disuse, and increasing circulation to the injured area.

If it hurts when you run, you should fall back to an activity (e.g. walking, or slow running) that makes use of the same muscles and tendons without causing pain.

Rick had a swollen and inflamed tendon behind his knee. He had hyper-extended his right leg running fast down a steep hill. At first he tried resting until the pain went away, When he resumed running his injury immediately returned. He then changed his approach. He walked at a quick pace, until his knee started to hurt. He then slowed to a pace that didn't hurt, and he maintained that pace for a week The next week he walked a little faster at a pace that didn't hurt. Each successive week he slowly increased his pace, always staying below the threshold of pain. After six weeks he was running at his pre-injury pace.

Rick healed his injury. because he maintained muscle strength, and increased the circulation in the injured area of his leg thru light exercise.

The Great outdoors

1. Terrain   "Don't you find running boring?" "What do you think about when you run?" These are questions I've heard from non-runners who envision me doing endless laps around a track. An outdoor track is where most of us start our running careers.
It has several advantages:
- It's built for running and is easy on feet and legs
- It's not hilly
- There is no vehicular traffic
- It is a measured distance, making it easy to chart progress

One major disadvantage - it can be dull! If you're just a beginner, you won't run long enough to get bored, but once you get up to two miles and you start to forget whether you did, 7, 8 or 9 laps, it's time to seek alternative running routes.

A run over macadam paths through a scenic park is ideal. Many parks have running trails with marked distances. Alley Pond Park in Eastern Queens, New York has marked trails, soft macadam paths, hills for variety of workouts and scenery for the soul.

If your distance should increase beyond five miles, you will find yourself doing repetitive loops and you may seek alternative running routes. You will go out on the roads, along beaches, through woods and urban and suburban neighborhoods, encountering auto and bike traffic, other people, and dogs. These options are discussed later in this book; the following observations deal strictly with terrain.

- **<u>Surfaces</u>**
  Running on concrete is hard on the legs. If black-top or Macadam is available on the same route, choose the softer surface

Running on sand puts more stress on your calf muscles. You may find your calf muscles are sore after a run in the sand.

Don't fun barefoot through fine sand. I once ran on a beach on the Gulf Coast where the sand was vey fine and, in doing so, "sand-papered" the skin off my toes.

Grassy surfaces provide good shock absorption but tend to be uneven, often hiding ankle-turning potholes.

A hard dirt path is smooth but soft enough for shock absorption. If the path is thru a wooded area it may contain foot-catching roots.

- **Hills**
  Running up hills is a good way to build endurance. Running down hills can be exhilarating but tough on the knees. Down hill running should be avoided if you have problems with your knees.

- **Embankments**
  There are subtle embankments along the shoulders of some roads and on the high tide water line of beaches. A run over this type of terrain places horizontal forces on knee tendons and ligaments. If the road is closed to traffic (as it would be for some races) , the best place to run is along the crown of the road– on the centerline.

- **Cliffside Beaches**
  You are on a business trip and you brought your running gear with you, Your hotel commands a magnificent view or the ocean from the top of a steep cliff. You descend to the beach and start your run.

As you run you fail to notice the incoming tide as it gradually narrows the beach. Later, you are miles from your starting point. On one side of you is a steep rocky cliff and on the other side is a turbulent ocean and a rapidly disappearing beach. There is no stairway nearby. You are in trouble.

If you run along a rocky beach, check the tides and the exit options before you start.

Forest Paths

You enjoy running thru the shady woods, on soft paths, with beautiful scenery. Your foot catches on a tree root and you sprain your ankle. You are immobilized in an isolated wood and only *you* know where your are.

Don't run alone in the woods or, if you do, inform someone of your run plan and estimated time of return. Mark your path as you go and leave plenty of daylight time for your return.

There are other potential problems with forest running; Poison Ivy, snakes and bears, but these are minor compared to what we can do to ourselves.

Snow and ice Covered Surfaces

I love running when falling snow covers the landscape with a white and quiet beauty.

Here are some guidelines I've found useful for Winter running.

- Slip on a pair of Yaktrax. These are the pedestrian equivalent of snow tires. Originally made for senior citizens they slip over your walking or running shoes and give you unbelievable traction on snow and ice. They can be purchased online or in most running stores.

- Waffle soles have better traction in snow than ripple or smooth soles but are slippery on ice.

Break new snow rather than use existing snow paths which tend to be icy and uneven.

Be wary of snow covered ice which can be found on wheel tracks on roads, windblown snow on sidewalks, or on sun exposed down-hills.

Slow your pace and run in small shuffling steps. This is no time for speed work.

If you slip and feel yourself going down, relax and take a rolling tumble. I once performed a frantic ice dance in an attempt to stay erect. I fell anyway and pulled a calf muscle. I was out of commission for a week.

When the snow has been around for a few days and the deep freeze has settled in, you will find very few safe outdoor running areas. Some exceptions:

- Industrial parking lots which are the first areas to be plowed and salted so that the work force can park.

- Shopping mall parking lots

If you'd rather run indoors:

- Long indoor hallways found in some industrial plants and schools.

- Sheltered passages thru large shopping malls. The Roosevelt Field Mall on Long Island opens early so that walkers and runners can walk and run before the stores open. The coffee shops are also open for post-run breakfast.

- Indoor tracks and health club treadmills, if you can stand the monotony.

Weather Unless you live in a mild, dry climate, and you run four to six days a week, you cannot avoid rain, snow, heat and cold. You can dress for rain and snow, but you can undress only so much when it's hot.

Running in the heat If sweating was an Olympic event, I would be a lock for a medal; possibly a silver or gold. After four consecutive days of hot weather running my weight would be down by five pounds; an apparent loss of 17,500 calories in spite of my 4000 calorie a day diet. After a two day rest, I'd regain the lost weight.

I regained my weight because most of my weight loss was water, and my hot weather runs had left me dehydrated. I discovered this after I started weighing myself before and after a run. If you try this, make sure you're naked and dry both times you get on the scale.

On hot days, I would be six pounds lighter after a six mile run. Water weighs about a pound a pint Six pounds represents a loss of six pints or three quarts of water. Major league pitchers have been known to lose ten pounds (five quarts) in nine innings!

Doctors say that when the temperature reaches the mid 90's sedentary people should drink a gallon of water a day, and active people should drink more. Most would find it difficult to drink that much water, and impossible to retain it. Chronic dehydration in warm weather is a common condition among athletes. They'll complain that... *"The heat doesn't bother me until two or three days have passed, and then I begin to feel fatigued and listless."*

Dehydration is more than uncomfortable; it can kill you. Symptoms of dehydration are feelings of fatigue, sometimes accompanied by night-time leg cramps. Symptoms of severe dehydration are heat stroke and death. Heat stroke cuts off blood flow to the brain, and impairs thinking. Just when you need your brain to tell you to stop running, it's no longer functioning.

S troke *def.* **A stroke is the sudden death of brain cells in a localized area due to inadequate blood flow**. Brain cells need oxygen and get their oxygen from red corpuscles in the blood stream. No blood flow, no oxygen. Most strokes are caused by clots which block blood flow, or hemorrhages, which rupture blood vessels, cutting off flow to areas of the brain.

Hyperthermia is the medical term for heat stroke.
Translation: **hyper:**   excessive or over
        thermia: heat
... or in English, ***over-heated***. But you knew that, didn't you?

Sweat glands draw water from the bloodstream. When the blood stream runs low on water, the victim stops sweating, blood pressure drops, and blood thickens. Low blood pressure can't push the thickened blood through the capillaries and heat stroke ensues.

In the 1984 Olympic Games, Gabriella Anderson-Scheiss neared the finish dazed and wobbly. The left side of her body was sagging. and she collapsed at the finish line. The diagnosis was hyperthermia.

Alberto Salazar, a three time winner of the NYC Marathon, was known to "save time" by passing up water stops.. In 1982 he won the Boston Marathon by seconds. He collapsed at the end, was immersed in a tub of ice water, and received 6 liters of water intraveously, a standard treatment for hyperthermia. Had he slowed down to drink, he would have lost the race, but without the special attention he received, he might have died.

Bob was member of our athletic club until he transferred to Reston Virginia. He trained to run a ten mile race. On race day the temperature and humidity were in the nineties. .They found Bob, and another runner lying dead in a wooded area just off the race course. Bob's goal was a PR for distance, the other man a PR for time. The autopsies confirmed that both men died of heat stroke.

When it it safe to run? A great deal of attention has been given to this question because there have been fatalities of high school and college athletes, and military trainees who were pushed beyond their limits in hot weather.

The military service uses a special thermometer designed to sense, absorb, and radiate heat much like the human body. Direct readings from this thermometer indicate whether or not heavy physical exercise should be permitted or curtailed.

The National Weather Service uses a Temperature-Humidity Index (THI) as an indicator of human discomfort. When the THI is 75, most people feel uncomfortable. When the THI is 80 or above, the discomfort is acute. Various combinations of temperature and humidity will yield the same THI readings. Examples of this are shown in the table below

THI = 75		THI = 80	
Temp. (Deg F)	Rel. Hum.(%)	Temp. (Deg F)	Rel. Hum.(%)
76	91	82	93
85	33	91	38
96	1	100	8

More information is available in a chart published in the National Weather Service Operation Manual which labels ranges of THI for relative safety for heavy exercise. (see THI Index chart)

THI under 75 = Safe;
THI between 75 and 79 = Alert
THI 80 or above = Danger

As a general rule, a runner should never strive for a personal record in either distance *or* pace when the THI approaches 75. Running should be slowed and distance reduced when the THI is between 75 and 79, and curtailed when the THI exceeds 80.

Some body types can tolerate heat better than others. Endomorphs

(rounded shape) and Mesomorphs(heavily muscular) do not tolerate heat as well as people with thin angular bodies (ectomorphs.)

Other Heat Induced Maladies

Heat Exhaustion (Heat Prostration) Symptoms are fatigue, sometimes accompanied by nausea or fainting. This condition differs from heat stroke in that the runner continues to sweat, often profusely. Recovery is quick when the runner moves to a shady area and reclines, with feet up and head down.

Heat Cramps are painful muscle spasms that can leave your muscles sore for hours. They occur after strenuous exercise in hot weather. The cause is believed to be electrolytic imbalance in the blood supply through the loss of water and minerals to the affected muscle. There are sport drinks available that will replace some of the minerals lost to hot weather running. Read the label, and avoid those that contain sugar because sweet liquids are slow to deliver relief. They remain in the stomach longer than drinks that don't contain sugar.

The writer experienced calf cramps in the final two miles of the Boston Marathon. It was warm and dry and my body sweat dried quickly, leaving salt deposits on my face, arms and legs. Those salts should have been in my blood stream instead of on the surface of my skin. As soon as my calf went into spasm, I'd slow my pace and the cramps would stop. Then I'd pick up my pace and the cramps would return. I'd been drinking only water and nothing to replace my lost electrolytes. With only four miles left in the race, it was too late to switch drinks.

A friend had the same experience in the New York Marathon. He lost his essential minerals by sitting in a steam room the day before the race. His calf cramp experience was similar to mine. I learned later that the salt we were missing was potassium chloride; found in tomatoes, bananas, strawberries, watermelons, and Sea Salt.

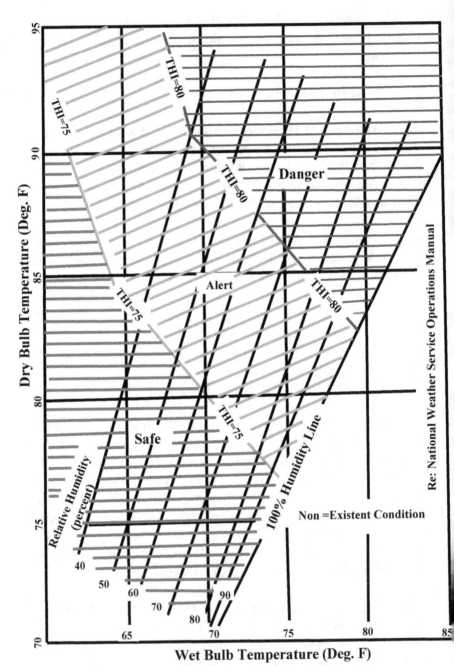

THI Index = (Wet Bulb Temp +Dry Bulb Temp.) X (0.4)+15

The Sling Psychrometer

When the weather is warm, it's important for you to know the Temperature Humidity Index (THI) The THI is measured with an instrument called the Sling Psychromter. It's a fancy name used to describe two thermometers mounted on a board, where one thermometer has wet gauze covering the mercury bulb.

A chain is attached to the board, and the person making the measurement takes hold of the chain and "slings" the board in a circular motion. When the humidity is low, water evaporates from the wet bulb, thereby cooling it, and the wet bulb thermometer will read a lower temperature than the dry bulb thermometer. The difference in temperatures determines the THI which can picked off a chart or plugged into the formula at the bottom of the chart. If the humidity is high, there will be little or no evaporation, and the two thermometers will have similar readings. Look at the chart. A dry bulb reading of 85 and a wet bulb reading of 80 indicates a humidity between 90 and 100 percent; a dangerous environment for heavy exercise.

The THI reading in the morning is usually very different than a reading in the late afternoon. Summer mornings on the East Coast of the US have high humidity and temperatures in the 70's. Afternoon temperatures may top 80 and the humidity will be much lower than in the morning. The Weather Bureau's reported THI may be "stale" by the time you decide to run. To get a timely reading you can buy your own Sling Psychrometer on the internet for about $60. Take your measurements in the shade because that's the way the weather bureau does it, and the chart and formula is based on temperatures measured in the shade. Our summer runs from our gym at work were preceded by a THI measurement, followed by a posting of green, yellow or red "flags"; pieces of day glow colored cardboard posted on our bulletin board.

A hot Marathon

You've increased your mileage base, and the mileage of your long runs. You sent your application, along with the entry fee, to the NY Road Runners, hoping you'll be one of the 65,000 runners selected. You get the good news you've been waiting for.. You rent a bus to take you and your friends to the race.

On Race Day the weather report is predicting a "Red Day." (THI 80 or above.) you know it's dangerous to run in the heat, but you've invested a lot of time and money, so you will go to the starting line convinced that you can deal with the situation. A true story follows.

Race Day

The weather prediction was bad, but even though the humidity was high, it was overcast and there was no sunlight. We were standing in the starting area at the base of the Verrazano Bridge. The air was so thick you couldn't see the bridge towers and then, just before the canon went off, the sun appeared, shining through the fog. There was a collective moan from thousands of runners. We all knew it wasn't going to be a fun day.

This wasn't my first marathon. I was an experienced runner and I knew what I had to do; slow my pace, drink lots of water, and douse my body with water at every water stop. Volunteers provided Ice cubes and I put some in my cap and put the cap on my head. I rubbed ice on the back of my neck, behind my knees and on my face and forearms.

My training investment was a strong incentive to finish but I had another reason; we had bets on our finish times. To win, you had to come close to your predicted finish time. Previous winners had finished within 30 seconds of their prediction. For a three and one half hour marathon, a 30 second prediction represents an accuracy of about 0.24 percent. Every year 2 to 3 people out of our group of 25 would finish within seconds of their prediction.

Our finish time predictions were made at a pasta loading dinner four days before the race. We ignored the long range weather forecast.

I knew, at the start, that I'd run much slower than my predicted time, and that the others in our betting pool would also run slower or even drop out of the race. I only had to finish, and I would win the $50.

Doug, showed superior intelligence by dropping out on First Avenue near the 18 mile mark. He walked into the nearest bar,

"What'll you have?" asked the bartender.
" Give me a beer"

As the bartender plunked the beer on the counter, Doug reached into the front of his shorts and retrieved a very wet twenty dollar bill. The bartender waved his hand away from the money, and said:

" It's on the house."

Doug had dropped out and couldn't win the pool. The only one who came close was Susan, and it was her first marathon. She ran slower (and smarter) than all of us. I was off my pre-diction by 45 minutes, having run a personal worst (PW). Most were off by half an hour. Susan was close to her 5:30 predic-tion and she won the $50

On the ride home, I sat between Walter and Bob. My head swiveled from one to the other as each repeatedly took turns saying "never again", "never again". I kept my mouth shut be-cause I didn't believe them. A week later the three of us en-tered the Jersey Shore marathon *"...to make up for our lousy performance in NY"*. How that turned out, is another story.

Hot Weather Running Summary

Do not run in hot weather if:

- If the Temperature Humidity Index (THI) is 75 or higher
- You, or any in your family has a history of Heart Disease
- If you haven't had a recent Stress Test.
- If you are overweight or very muscular.
- If you do not sweat freely.
- If you have a fever, are fatigued or dehydrated.
- If you have donated blood in the past three weeks.
- If for any reason, you find the effort uncomfortable.

When the weather is hot be aware that...

- ...The mornings will be cool, but humidity will be high.
- ...Late afternoons will have lower humidity and a breeze.
- ...A run in the rain will cool you, and you won't catch cold if you keep moving. Avoid thunderstorms.
- ...A run after sunset will be the coolest run of the day..
- ... you should hydrate, hydrate, hydrate. Carry water for drinking. Pour water on your head, back and chest.

If you run in the rain or the heat, non-runners will tell you you're crazy., but runners may follow your example; good or bad!

After coming in from a pouring rain, my daughter Jeanne stood in the foyer, dripping wet, T-shirt and shorts sticking to her skin, and hair totally disheveled. My wife looked at her and said **"I don't understand you."** Jeanne said, **"Mom , your husband, my father, is out there, running in the rain, right now."**

Cold Weather Running

Winter can be the best time of the year to run. A runner moving at a seven minute per mile pace will generate enough body heat to stay comfortable on a 45 degree day dressed only in shorts and a T-shirt. Leg coverings may not be needed until the temperature drops into the 20's. A runner's body type and pace will determine how much clothing to wear for a comfortable Winter run..

A runner may look funny wearing a T-shirt, shorts, gloves and a hat; but a veteran runner values comfort over appearance. Experience is a good teacher, although sometimes painful. In the interest of sparing you some pain, the following hints are offered:

1. **Protect Your Extremities** Fingers are the first place where you'll feel the cold. Cotton mittens (not gloves) will be warm enough until the temperature drops into the teens and then an extra layer of protection will be needed. Thermal mitten liners made by Damart (New Hampshire) allow sweat to pass thru the fabric while keeping hands warm and dry.

   I seldom wore a hat in Winter, until I started to run. Then I found what hat wearers knew all along; a hat helps keep the rest of the body warm because 25 to 40 percent of body heat is radiated from the head. A wool cap pulled down over the ears and neck or rolled up to sit on top of the head provides flexibility for changing conditions. A ski mask is too warm most of the time and may severely restrict vision.

   Males are vulnerable in the groin. Nylon shorts are comfortable most of the year, but can cause penile frostbite in Winter. Wool underwear or a wool sock, doubled over and pinned inside your shorts can save you from a painful experience. Wool retains body heat when wet, and should be worn during a cold rain when the temperature is close to freezing..

Winter Wind Air temperature is only half of the story. At 20 degrees with no wind , you will feel as warm as you would at 35 degrees in a 10 mile per hour head wind. This effect is known as the "wind chill" factor and is caused by the rapid conduction of heat from the skin by the cold air mass.

You generate your own wind when you run through an air mass. On a day with no wind, a runner moving at an eight minute pace generates his own 7.5 mile-an-hour head wind. This wont happen on a treadmill because you're running in place thru a static air mass.

If you're running at an eight minute pace and you run into a 10 mile per hour head wind the resultant effect is a head wind of 17.5 miles per hour. When you reverse direction, the wind will be at your back, pushing you, and the effective wind speed will be the difference between 10 miles per hour and 7.5 miles per hour or 2.5 miles per hour. If you're comfortable running into the wind, you may feel over -dressed when the wind is at your back.

You can adapt to the weather with the right type of clothing. A jacket with a front zipper can be opened when the wind is at your back, and closed when you run into the wind. A hat can be removed, or rolled up, when the wind is behind you, and pulled down over your ears when wind is in your face.

Start your run into the wind and return with the wind at your back. If you start with the wind at your back you may sweat heavily on the way out. You will be wet when you turn around, and the wind chill will be more severe.

Clothing Wool retains body heat when wet but may be too warm. You'll be more comfortable wearing wool in a cold rainfall than you would be wearing cotton or nylon which, when wet, will be as cold as the rain. Gortex permits the passage of sweat vapor out but blocks the passage of rain drops in; you may get wet, but you'll stay warm.

Nose and Eyes My eyes tear when I run into a cold head wind. A pair of downhill ski goggles provide a neat solution to this problem. They do not fog over and afford good visibility with their wrap around lenses. The trick is to know when to wear them and when to leave them home.

There is a myth that cold air freezes the lungs. Doctors deny this, claiming that air is sufficiently warmed by the body before it reaches the bronchial tubes. Still. Some runners feel better with a handkerchief tied over their nose and mouth. This has multiple benefits: it pre-warms the input air, protects the lips from chapping, and keeps the nose warm.

Thunderstorms. "Don't be afraid", we were taught, "it's only thunder." Sorry, mom and dad, that was poor training. Every time you hear thunder, lightning has just struck something. If you are out in storm and are the highest object in an open area, that "something" could be you.

On my first summer as a novice golf caddy, I witnessed a lightning bolt tear a hole in the ground and strike a buried water pipe. The two older, more experienced caddies in our foursome dropped their golf clubs and ran. They knew that golf clubs, with their metal shafts, are excellent lightning rods.

On July 3rd, 2011, 54 year old Steve Rooney was standing in his yard, five feet from a Sycamore tree, when lightning struck the tree, traveled down the root system and struck Steve who died later that day. Steve had told his friends and family that he never worried about lightning because, when he was five years old, his 48 year old father George Rooney was killed by lightning, near the same tree, and he believed that "lightning never strikes twice."

This commonly held belief is contradicted by photos, taken on several different occasions, of lightning striking the Empire State Building in New York City. This building is the highest in the area and is the most likely target whenever a storm is brewing.

I like running in a warm rain, but when I hear thunder, I seek shelter near a *group* of objects higher than me (trees, buildings, etc.) . If you take shelter under a *single* tree, you and the tree, are potential lightning rods. If you can get indoors, do so! Since most storms pass quickly, you wont be delayed for long.

Blizzards A blizzard is a blinding snowstorm with high winds and snowdrifts that obscure roads and landmarks . It's easy to get lost in a blizzard, even in familiar territory. Never set out in a blizzard and if you are running when one develops, end your run as quickly as possible.

44

Night Runs Most people who work daylight hours will run in the dark. If you work for a company that has facilities for lunch-time exercise, you should run in the daytime and avoid the dark.

If you run in the dark, avoid sidewalks. Tree roots lift paving blocks, cold weather leaves holes in pavement, and children leave bicycles on sidewalks. Run on the street, near the curb, facing traffic, and watch for rocks, bottles, and cans. Wear bright, reflective clothing and a camper's headlamp. You may look great in your navy blue sweats, but unless your eyes glow in the dark, you'll be virtually invisible on a night time run.

If night running in the street is your only option, then re-read the section about running in traffic, and insure you're visible.

Once, while driving at night, I almost hit one of my running friends. When I got home, I called my friend and told him about his limited visibility. Soon after, we both bought reflective leg bands, head bands and vests and made sure that we wore tastelessly bright clothing on our night time runs.

When you run in daylight, you look where you'll plant your next footstep and you automatically adjust for the step ahead. If the road is so dark that you can't see where your foot will land, your foot impact will be hard and uneven and you risk taking a tumble. I've tripped and fallen in broad daylight twice. Both times I had taken my eyes off the road in front of me. I might as well have been running in the dark.

A High School rubberized track is the safest venue for night time running; it's smooth, free of potholes, and has excellent shock absorption. Sometimes there's a game on the infield and the floodlights are on. I've run under these conditions and the spectators and players were never interested in watching me run; they were watching the game.

Traffic A study released in the early eighties stated that 85% of pedestrians hit by cars did not have a license to drive. It made sense because the victims, not being drivers, had no understanding of driver visibility or how long it could take for a moving two-ton vehicle to stop.

The New York Road Runners claim that 85% of NYC Marathon Runners have college degrees and are employed in middle class jobs. One could assume that most of them have driver's licenses and have some understanding of vehicle dynamics. Then why do runners do stupid things, either losing their lives as a result, or putting their safety in jeopardy? It may be due to a schizoid type of behavior I've sometimes observed in myself. As a pedestrian I can be inconsiderate of drivers and vice versa; forgetting each time that I occasionally switch roles.

In any case, I see too many runners who believe that the road was built for running, and, should a car come along, the driver will see them, change lanes, or stop on a dime. May they all rest in peace.

To keep from becoming a traffic statistic, consider the following:

- When you run on the road, run on the far left shoulder, facing traffic.

- Watch the approaching car and look at the driver. In one out of three times, the driver will be looking anywhere but the road in front of him; i.e. at a passenger, the girl across the street, or reading a book or newspaper; (I've seen it all.) Be ready to dive into the bushes.

- Wear clothing that is obnoxiously bright. Orange day-glow hats, headbands and shirts work well in the daytime especially against drab winter backgrounds. At night, pin reflective tape to your clothing, wear reflective vests, headbands and leg bands and yellow or white clothing. Wear a headlamp so you can see, and be seen.

- As you run up a hill, be aware that the driver on the other side of the hill will be surprised to see you; that is, even if he is looking at the road. In this situation you will be safer and more visible on the right shoulder, with traffic behind you, until you go over the hill. Then, very cautiously, get back on the left shoulder. The same is true if the road takes a sharp turn to the left. Temporarily move to the right side of the road until you are past the turn.

- If you are running on the left, and you approach an intersection where a driver is waiting to turn onto the road, he won't be looking at you. He will be looking away from you, in the direction of oncoming traffic. Never cross in front of his car, always cross behind it.

- I was in a road race where the driver parked his car sideways across a narrow bridge as a practical joke with the intention of blocking the runners. We stepped over the hood and roof of his car and probably ruined his paint job. The driver was stupid, and we weren't much smarter, but it was a race, and it was quickest solution to a problem.

- If an oncoming car seems to be aiming for you, the driver may be having some fun, thinking he'll scare you. *Be scared*. The driver has just demonstrated immaturity and bad judgment. Assume he'll miscalculate and hit you. Jump to the side of the road.

- Be extra careful during heavy precipitation or fog when neither the driver nor you have a clear view of the road. Always assume you're invisible.

- Finally, do nothing to take your concentration off the road. It's a bad place for daydreaming.

Pedestrians   Most of us run faster than we realize, and we can startle people, especially if we approach them quickly from behind. If someone in front of you is walking or running in the same direction, he won't see or hear you coming. Let him know you're there. In a gentle, but loud, voice announce **"Runner coming, excuse me."**

This doesn't always work. There were days when I would run at 5:00 am because there was no other time available. On one of those days, I was running on a lonely stretch of road, with no lighting, and woods on both sides. In the distance I saw a man, walking in front of me, heading the same way, and carrying his suit jacket over his arm.

Considering the time, and the way he was dressed, I thought it unusual, but felt the need to tell him I was there. **"Good Morning"** I yelled. **"Yow!!"** he screamed, as he jumped a foot in the air. **"I'm sorry, I didn't want to frighten you."**, I said. I wondered what he was doing there at 5:00 am. I'm sure he was wondering the same about me.

Man's Best Friend   I'm part owner of a dog. I own the part that eats and the other end where the vet sticks his needle. I like dogs and I'm not afraid of them. A dog will know if you're afraid from your body language, and will view you as a potential threat.

A dog will react, especially if you appear to be running away from him, which the dog will take as a sign of fear. As you pass in front of a house where a dog lives, the dog will bark and, if he is loose, will give chase.

Stop running, turn around, point your finger at the dog, and in a loud commanding voice, yell **"Go home!"** This has always worked for me except once, when the owner came out of the house and yelled at the dog in Chinese. The dog put his tail between his legs and went into the house. I had no way of knowing that the dog was Chinese.

I've run thousands of miles, encountered many dogs, and never had to do anything to hurt or injure an animal.

Cherish The Women I have three daughters who run, but they seldom run alone. Two run with friends and one runs with Man's Best Friend, a big Golden Retriever. I had a co-worker who ran every morning with his two dogs. On days when he tried to skip his run they would go into the bedroom and wake him up.

Not everyone can run with company. If you run alone, be aware that there are creeps out there who will try to take advantage of you. Save that polite "Good Morning" for another woman. The wrong man might take your greeting as a sign of encouragement.

A few words of caution:

- Don't make it easy for someone to enter your house while you're gone. Lock the windows and doors. Keep your key in your shoe.

- Try to run at a busy time of day and avoid isolated areas. Tell your room mate where you're going and when you'll return.

- Vary your route from day to day and reverse direction once in a while. This will change the times that you pass various landmarks.

- Do not appear frightened. Run with your head erect and pay attention. If you look scared you'll encourage an attack.

- If confronted, run, yell, feign insanity, or nausea, or any action which might discourage an attacker.

- A physical response requires training, knowledge, and self confidence.. A hard kick to the groin must be done swiftly, forcefully and with surprise in order to be effective.

- While your attacker is trying to recover it's time to run away. If you stay, you could lose a physical struggle to a stronger, heavier male, and the possibility of serious injury or death.

Epilogue

" You've been telling me to run, but I can't because I have ... (fill in your condition,)"

As a spectator at the NYC Marathon, I've seen the following....

- At the end of the 26.2 mile race, a runner removed his leg prosthesis, and turned it upside down to empty some accumulated water. A passing biker, distracted by the sight, steered his bike into a nearby tree.

- One year I was unable to run, and felt sorry for myself. I stood at the 24 mile mark and watched blind runners, tethered by ropes to volunteers, on the way to breaking three hours, for a 26.2 mile effort. My self pity evaporated

- I saw a double amputee, pushing herself on a skateboard. She finished the 26.2 miles many hours after the last runner.

In local races, I've seen...

- ...men and women in wheelchairs designed for racing, compete against other wheelchair racers, while covering the course in half the finish time of the winning runner.

- ...leg amputees (some double), wearing prosthetics designed specifically for racing, running in the 10K Aspire Race The Aspire Race is managed by the Greater Long Island Running Club and the race income benefits leg amputees..

Race Walking is easier on the knees and can be every bit as aerobic as running. I've been passed, more than once, by race walkers, moving at a 7:30 pace while I was running at an 8:00 minute pace. I'd pick up my pace and try to catch them. Never did.

"When you stop moving, they through dirt on you"
Sid Richfield

Sid's point is obvious; you need to be active to continue living. If you're breathing, and have a pulse, a doctor will say you're alive. But you can breath, have a heart beat, and be comatose. Medically you would be defined as being alive, but you wouldn't really be "living."

To keep living you need to keep moving because...

- When a muscle isn't used, it weakens and atrophies. The weakened muscle is able to do less, so you do less, and the muscle gets weaker, so you do less, and the muscle gets weaker, etc. More simply, the less you do, the less you're able to do. It's a downhill spiral.

- Being physically active can be enjoyable, and your activity will raise the quality of your life. Walking, hiking, ice or roller skating, biking, playing with your kids or grand kids, pick-up ball games, or just going for a stroll with your spouse or sweetheart, will keep you fit, and away from TV sit-coms, and other blather that passes for entertainment.

This book was about running for fitness. because running is an activity I love. There are many other activities you may enjoy while reaping the benefits.. If you think of exercise as work, you'll find excuses to avoid it. Instead, drop the word "exercise" from your vocabulary and substitute the name of your favorite physical activity.

You've heard **"Find a job you love, and you won't have to work a day in your life."** Similarly, **"Find a physical activity you love, and you won't have to exercise a day in your life." GO FOR IT!!**

OPTOMIZE YOUR RACES WITH FITNESS FACTORS

What is a Fitness Factor? A runner/mathematician discovered that a Fitness Factor (FF) could be calculated for every runner that could predict the runner's finish time for any distance. He derived a formula(1) that assigned a **FF** of 1000 to Olympic Gold Medal Winners and winners of the New York and Boston Marathons. He classified these athletes as World Class Runners. The rest of us have **FFs** lower than 1000.   Your **FF** depends on your aerobic condition, training, and natural ability. I found the **FF** calculation complex and time consuming. I needed a quicker and easier way to find my optimum race pace.   I wrote a computer program that allows anyone to easily find their Fitness Factor and optimal race pace from a set of tables. The tables that follow list Fitness Factors with race paces for a large range of paces and distances.

How can you use it to optimize your race performance? It allows you to select the optimum race pace for any distance. An optimum pace is *consistent* from start to finish.. Most runners tend to start fast and finish slow with the result that the early miles are taxing, and the later miles uncomfortable. Despite the extra effort and discomfort, the runner's finish time will be the same as if the runner ran the whole race at an *even* pace.

To use the tables, pick a distance you've recently raced and move across the table until you find the pace at which you ran that distance.   The number under your pace and across from your distance is your Fitness Factor. You will find that this **FF** will hold for all distances for which you had *adequately trained* and will predict the pace at which you can run these distances. When you plug in your **FF** for longer races the tables will tell you to run slower. You know your car burns more fuel per mile at higher speeds. Similarly your muscles consume more fuel (glycogen) per mile at faster paces. *If you "cheat" by starting too fast , you will deplete your glycogen stores, slow down in the later miles, and finish with the time you would have had if you had run evenly and more comfortably.*

A1

Whenever I started too fast, I lost the time I'd saved, and was later passed by smarter runners. Some runners believe they should start fast and "put it in the bank." When I held to my **FF** pace, I passed those runners in the later miles and finished ahead of them

Running slower than you can, is difficult because it goes against your racing instincts. Dr. George Sheehan would run marathons with his sons, who never listened to his advice to start slow. He would try to be last at the start, and when he passed them late in the race, he would wave his handkerchief at them. He was ten years my senior when he passed me at mile 20 in the Jersey Shore Marathon. The Fitness Factor Tables will allow you to find. an optimal pace without doing any complex math. Using the tables is fast and easy.

Example: Last, week, Bob ran 5 miles at a pace of 6.1 minutes (6:06.) His **FF** (from the tables) is **716**. Bob has been training for a half marathon (13.1 miles).. What pace can he expect to average?

Answer: Using his **FF** of 716 and a distance of 13 miles (slightly low), the closest **FF** to 716 in the table is 718. This would give him a pace of 6.5 (6:30) for 13 miles and a finish time of about one hour and twenty five minutes (1:25.) Note that Bob should run 24 seconds slower per mile than he did when he ran his five mile race.

Fitness Factor Tables covering race distances from the mile to the marathon are in the pages that follow. It includes paces from 4:00 minutes/mile to 12+ minutes/mile.

---

(1) To do it the hard way, use these formulas instead of the tables

$$FF = (3785/ P)* D^{.0689}$$
Where **D = Distance in Kilometers or Miles/0.62137**
P = Pace (in min/Km); FF= Fitness Factor

A2

Fitness Factor as a Function of Distance and Pace
FF = 1000 is World Class

Pace .... In Minutes and Seconds per Mile

Miles	4:00	4:06	4:12	4:18	4:24	4:30	4:36	4:42	4:48	4:54
1	978	954	931	910	889	869	850	832	815	798
2		1001	977	954	932	912	892	873	855	837
3*			1004	981	959	937	917	898	879	861
4				1001	978	956	935	916	896	878
5					993	971	950	930	910	892
6*					1006	983	962	941	922	903
7						994	972	952	932	913
8						1003	981	960	940	921
9*							989	968	948	929
10							996	975	955	935
11							1003	982	961	942
12*								988	967	947
13								993	972	952
14								998	977	957
15								1003	982	962
16*									986	966
17									990	970
18									994	974
19*									998	978
20									1002	981
21									1005	984
22										988
23										991
24										994
25										996
26										999

* 5K = 3.1M, 10K = 6.2M, 15K = 9.3M, 20K = 12.4M, 25K = 15.5M,
30K = 15.5M, 35K = 18.5M, 42K = 26.2M

A3

Fitness Factor as a Function of Distance and Pace

FF = 1000 is World Class

Pace ...in Minutes and Seconds per Mile

Miles	5:00	5:06	5:12	5:18	5:24	5:30	5:36	5:42	5:48	5:54
1	782	767	752	738	724	711	698	686	674	663
2	820	804	789	774	760	746	733	720	707	695
3*	844	827	811	796	781	767	753	740	727	715
4	861	844	828	812	797	782	768	755	742	729
5	874	857	840	82.4	809	795	780	767	753	741
6*	885	868	851	835	819	805	790	776	763	750
7	894	877	860	844	828	813	799	785	771	758
8	903	885	868	852	836	821	806	792	778	765
9*	910	892	875	859	843	827	813	798	785	771
10	917	899	881	865	849	833	818	804	790	777
11	923	905	887	871	854	839	824	809	795	782
12*	928	910	893	876	860	844	829	814	800	787
13	933	915	898	881	64	849	833	819	805	791
14	938	920	902	885	869	853	838	823	809	795
15	943	924	906	889	873	857	842	827	813	799
16*	947	938	910	893	877	861	845	831	816	802
17	951	932	914	397	880	864	849	834	820	806
18	955	936	918	901	884	868	852	837	823	809
19*	958	939	921	904	887	871	856	840	826	812
20	962	943	925	907	890	874	859	843	829	815
21	965	946	928	910	893	877	861	846	832	818
22	968	949	931	913	896	880	864	849	834	820
23	971	952	934	916	899	883	867	852	837	823
24	974	955	936	919	902	885	869	854	839	825
25	976	957	939	921	904	888	872	857	842	828
26	979	960	941	924	907	890	874	859	844	830

* 5K = 3.1M, 10K = 6.2M, 15K = 9.3M, 20K = 12.4M, 25K = 15.5M,
30K = 15.5M, 35K = 18.5M, 42K = 26.2M

A4

Fitness Factor as a Function of Distance and Pace
FF = 1000 is World Class

Pace .... In Minutes and Seconds per Mile

Miles	6:00	6:06	6:12	6:18	6:24	6:30	6:36	6:42	6;48	6:54
1	652	641	631	621	611	602	593	584	575	567
2	684	673	662	651	641	631	622	612	603	595
3*	703	692	680	670	659	649	639	630	620	611
4	717	705	694	683	672	662	652	642	633	624
5	728	716	705	694	683	672	662	652	643	633
6*	738	725	714	702	691	681	672	660	651	641
7	745	733	721	710	699	688	678	668	658	648
8	752	740	728	716	705	694	684	674	664	654
9*	758	746	794	722	711	700	689	679	669	659
10	764	751	719	729	716	705	694	684	674	664
11	769	756	744	732	721	710	699	689	678	669
12*	774	761	749	737	725	714	703	693	683	673
13	778	765	753	741	729	718	707	697	686	676
14	782	769	757	145	733	722	711	700	690	680
15	786	771	760	748	736	725	714	703	693	683
16*	789	776	764	751	740	728	717	707	696	686
17	792	779	767	755	743	731	720	710	699	689
18	795	782	770	758	746	734	723	712	702	692
19*	798	785	773	760	749	737	726	715	705	694
20	801	788	775	763	751	740	728	718	707	697
21	804	791	778	766	754	742	731	720	709	699
22	807	793	781	768	756	745	733	722	712	701
23	809	796	783	771	758	737	735	725	714	704
24	811	798	785	773	761	749	738	727	716	706
25	814	800	787	775	763	751	740	729	718	708
26	816	803	790	777	765	753	742	731	720	709

* 5K = 3.1M, 10K = 6.2M, 15K = 9.3M, 20K = 12.4M, 25K = 15.5M,
30K = 15.5M, 35K = 18.5M, 42K = 26.2M

A5

Fitness Factor as a Function of Distance and Pace
FF = 1000 is World Class

Pace ...in Minutes and Seconds per Mile

Miles	7:00	7:06	7:12	7:18	7:24	7:30	7:36	7:42	7:48	7:54
1	559	551	543	536	529	521	515	508	501	495
2	586	578	570	562	554	547	540	533	526	519
3*	603	594	586	578	570	562	555	548	541	534
4	615	606	598	589	582	574	566	559	552	545
5	624	615	607	599	591	583	575	568	560	553
6*	632	623	615	606	598	590	582	575	567	560
7	639	630	621	613	604	596	588	581	573	566
8	645	636	627	618	610	602	594	586	579	571
9*	650	641	632	623	615	607	599	591	583	576
10	655	646	637	628	619	611	603	595	588	580
11	659	650	641	632	623	615	607	599	592	584
12*	663	654	645	636	627	619	611	603	595	580
13	667	657	648	639	631	622	614	606	598	591
14	670	661	652	643	634	625	617	609	601	594
15	673	664	655	646	637	628	620	612	604	597
16*	676	667	658	649	640	631	623	615	607	599
17	679	670	660	651	642	634	626	617	610	602
18	682	672	663	654	645	636	628	620	612	604
19*	684	675	665	656	647	639	630	622	614	606
20	687	677	668	659	650	641	633	624	616	609
21	689	679	670	661	652	643	635	626	618	611
22	691	682	672	663	654	645	637	628	620	613
23	693	684	674	665	656	647	639	630	622	614
24	696	686	676	667	658	649	641	632	624	616
25	697	688	678	669	660	651	642	634	626	618
26	699	690	680	671	662	653	644	636	628	620

* 5K = 3.1M, 10K = 6.2M, 15K = 9.3M, 20K = 12.4M, 25K = 15.5M,
30K = 15.5M, 35K = 18.5M, 42K = 26.2M

A6

Fitness Factor as a Function of Distance and Pace
FF = 1000 is World Class

Pace .... In Minutes and Seconds per Mile

Miles	8:00	8:00	8:12	8:18	8:24	8:30	8:36	8:42	8:48	8:54
1	489	483	477	471	466	460	455	450	444	439
2	513	506	500	494	488	483	477	472	466	461
3*	527	521	514	508	502	496	491	485	479	474
4	538	531	525	518	512	506	500	495	489	483
5	546	539	533	526	510	514	508	502	497	491
6*	553	546	540	533	527	521	515	509	503	497
7	559	552	545	539	532	526	520	514	508	503
8	564	557	550	544	537	531	525	519	513	507
9*	569	562	555	548	542	535	529	523	517	511
10	573	566	559	552	546	539	533	527	521	515
11	577	570	563	556	549	543	536	530	524	518
12*	580	573	566	559	553	546	540	534	527	522
13	583	576	569	562	556	549	543	536	530	524
14	586	579	572	565	558	552	545	539	533	527
15	589	582	575	568	561	555	548	542	536	530
16*	592	584	577	570	564	557	551	544	538	532
17	594	587	580	573	566	559	553	546	540	534
18	597	589	582	575	568	562	555	549	542	536
19*	599	591	584	577	570	564	557	551	544	538
20	601	594	586	579	572	566	559	553	546	540
21	603	596	588	581	574	568	561	554	548	542
22	605	597	590	583	576	569	563	556	550	544
23	607	599	592	585	578	571	564	558	552	545
24	609	601	594	587	580	573	566	560	553	547
25	610	603	595	588	581	574	568	561	555	549
26	612	604	597	590	583	576	569	563	556	550

* 5K = 3.1M, 10K = 6.2M, 15K = 9.3M, 20K = 12.4M, 25K = 15.5M,
30K = 15.5M, 35K = 18.5M, 42K = 26.2M

A7

Fitness Factor as a Function of Distance and Pace

FF = 1000 is World Class

Pace ...in Minutes and Seconds per Mile

Miles	9:00	9:06	9:12	9:18	9:24	9:30	9:36	9:42	9:48	9:54
1	435	430	425	421	416	412	407	403	399	395
2	456	451	446	441	436	432	427	423	419	414
3*	469	464	459	454	449	444	439	435	430	426
4	478	473	468	463	458	453	448	444	439	435
5	486	480	475	470	465	460	455	450	446	441
6*	492	486	481	476	471	466	461	456	452	447
7	497	491	486	481	476	471	466	461	456	452
8	502	496	491	485	480	475	470	465	461	456
9*	506	500	495	489	484	479	474	469	464	460
10	509	504	498	493	488	482	477	473	468	463
11	513	507	501	496	491	486	481	476	471	466
12*	516	510	505	499	494	489	483	479	474	469
13	519	513	507	502	497	491	486	481	476	471
14	521	516	510	504	499	494	489	484	479	474
15	524	518	512	507	501	496	491	486	481	476
16*	526	520	515	509	504	498	493	488	483	478
17	528	522	517	511	506	500	495	490	485	480
18	530	525	519	513	508	502	497	492	487	482
19*	532	526	521	515	510	504	499	494	489	484
20	534	528	523	517	511	506	501	496	491	486
21	536	530	524	519	513	508	502	497	492	487
22	538	532	526	520	515	509	504	499	494	489
23	539	533	528	522	516	511	506	500	495	490
24	541	535	529	523	510	512	507	502	477	492
25	542	537	531	525	519	514	509	503	498	493
26	544	538	532	526	521	515	510	505	500	494

* 5K = 3.1M, 10K = 6.2M, 15K = 9.3M, 20K = 12.4M, 25K = 15.5M,
30K = 15.5M, 35K = 18.5M, 42K = 26.2M

A8

Fitness Factor as a Function of Distance and Pace

FF = 1000 is World Class

Pace .... In Minutes and Seconds per Mile

Miles	10:00	10:06	10:12	10:18	10:24	10:30	10:36	10:42	10:48	10:54
1	391	387	383	380	376	372	369	366	362	359
2	410	406	402	398	394	391	387	383	380	376
3*	422	418	414	410	406	402	398	394	391	387
4	430	426	422	418	414	410	406	402	398	395
5	437	433	428	424	420	416	412	408	405	401
6*	443	438	434	430	425	421	417	414	410	406
7	447	443	438	434	430	426	422	418	414	410
8	451	447	443	438	434	430	426	422	418	414
9*	455	451	446	442	438	433	429	425	421	417
10	458	454	449	445	441	437	432	428	424	421
11	461	457	452	448	444	439	435	431	427	423
12*	464	460	455	451	446	442	438	434	430	426
13	467	462	458	453	449	444	440	436	432	428
14	469	464	460	455	451	447	443	438	434	430
15	471	467	462	458	453	449	445	441	436	432
16*	473	469	464	460	455	451	447	442	438	434
17	475	471	466	462	457	453	449	444	440	436
18	477	473	468	463	459	455	450	446	442	438
19*	479	474	470	465	461	456	452	448	444	440
20	481	476	471	467	462	458	454	449	445	441
21	482	478	473	468	464	459	455	451	447	443
22	484	479	474	470	465	461	457	452	448	444
23	485	481	476	471	467	462	458	454	449	445
24	487	482	477	473	468	464	459	455	451	447
25	488	483	479	474	469	465	461	456	452	448
26	490	485	480	475	471	466	462	458	453	449

* 5K = 3.1M, 10K = 6.2M, 15K = 9.3M, 20K = 12.4M, 25K = 15.5M,
30K = 15.5M, 35K = 18.5M, 42K = 26.2M

A9

61

Fitness Factor as a Function of Distance and Pace									
FF = 1000 is World Class									
Pace .... In Minutes and Seconds per Mile									
	11:00	11:06	11:12	11:18	11:24	11:30	11:36	11:42	11:48	11:54
Miles									
1	356	352	349	346	343	340	337	334	331	329
2	373	370	366	363	360	357	354	351	348	345
3*	384	380	377	373	370	367	364	361	358	355
4	391	388	384	381	377	374	371	368	365	362
5	397	394	390	387	383	380	377	373	370	367
6*	402	399	395	392	388	385	381	378	375	372
7	407	403	399	396	392	389	386	382	379	376
8	410	407	403	399	396	392	389	386	383	379
9*	414	410	406	403	399	396	392	389	386	382
10	417	413	409	406	402	399	395	392	388	385
11	419	416	412	408	405	401	398	394	391	388
12*	422	418	414	411	407	404	400	397	393	390
13	424	420	417	413	409	406	402	399	396	392
14	426	423	419	415	411	408	404	401	398	394
15	428	425	421	417	413	410	406	403	399	396
16*	430	427	423	419	415	412	408	405	401	398
17	432	428	424	421	417	413	410	406	403	400
18	434	430	426	422	419	415	411	408	404	401
19*	436	432	428	424	420	417	413	409	406	403
20	437	433	429	425	422	418	414	411	407	404
21	439	435	431	427	423	419	416	412	409	405
22	440	436	432	428	425	421	417	414	410	407
23	441	437	433	430	426	422	418	415	411	408
24	443	439	435	431	427	423	420	416	413	409
25	444	440	436	432	428	425	421	417	414	410
26	445	441	437	433	429	426	422	418	415	411

* 5K = 3.1M, 10K = 6.2M, 15K = 9.3M, 20K = 12.4M, 25K = 15.5M,
30K = 15.5M, 35K = 18.5M, 42K = 26.2M

A10

62

Fitness Factor as a Function of Distance and Pace									
FF = 1000 is World Class									
Pace .... In Minutes and Seconds per Mile									
	12:00	12:06	12:12	12:18					
Miles									
1	326	323	321	318					
2	342	339	336	334					
3*	352	349	346	343					
4	359	356	353	350					
5	364	361	358	355					
6*	369	366	363	360					
7	373	370	367	364					
8	376	373	370	367					
9*	379	376	373	370					
10	382	379	376	373					
11	384	381	378	375					
12*	387	384	380	377					
13	389	386	383	379					
14	391	388	385	381					
15	393	390	386	383					
16*	395	391	388	385					
17	396	393	390	387					
18	398	394	391	388					
19*	399	396	393	389					
20	401	397	394	391					
21	402	399	395	392					
22	403	400	397	393					
23	405	401	398	395					
24	406	402	399	396					
25	407	403	400	397					
26	408	405	401	398	5:22 Marathon				
* 5K = 3.1M, 10K = 6.2M, 15K = 9.3M, 20K = 12.4M, 25K = 15.5M,									
30K = 15.5M, 35K = 18.5M, 42K = 26.2M									
				A11					

REFERENCES

IV.

1. Kenneth H. Cooper, M.D., M.P.H. "The Aeorobics Way" Bantam Books.

2. "Runner's World" Runner's World Magazine Co. 1400 Stierlin Road, Mountain View, California 94043

3. Shoe Saver (brand), Shoe Patch (Trademark) distributed by The KIWI Polish Co., Pottstown, Pennsylvania 19464

4. "Runner's World", October 1980, page 11.

5. "Dr. Sheehan on Running" Dr. George Sheehan, Simon and Shuster, New York.

6. "Stretching" Robert A. and Jean E. Anderson, P.O. Box 2734 Fullerton, California 92633

7. "Running for My Life" Robert E. Hood, Scouting Magazine October 1980

8. "The Complete Diet Guide For Runners and Other Athletes" by the editors of World Publications.

9. Carlton Fredericks, Nutritionist; 'Design for Living"

10. "Athletic Training and Conditioning" O. William Dayton The Ronald Press Company, New York

11. "Fitness Factor Tables" generated using BASIC Interpreter Software; designed and coded by George Erkmann

V. Illustration Credits
1. Cover lettering....Jeanne Rafferty
2. All Illustrations ... Christopher Erkmann